Contents

Getting started

Textiles – fibres, fabrics and thread – can be painted, dyed, woven, wrapped, sewn, knotted, glued and even moulded. The projects in this book introduce a whole range of textile crafts.

Which stitch?

A few of the projects in this book require basic sewing skills. If you don't already know how, practise the easy stitches below.

Running Stitch – the basic stitch for joining two pieces of fabric together.

1 Thread needle and knot the end of your thread. Push needle to the front of the fabric, from the back. Pull thread up until the knot tugs.

2 A little further along, push the needle back down. Continue sewing in and out, making even stitches.

3 When you reach the end, sew round and round through the last stitch, then cut off the thread.

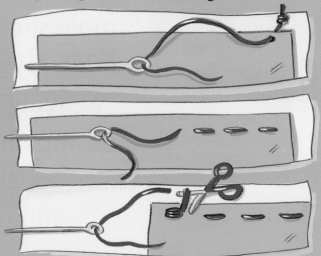

Oversewing – to neaten an edge or join two fabrics together at their edges.

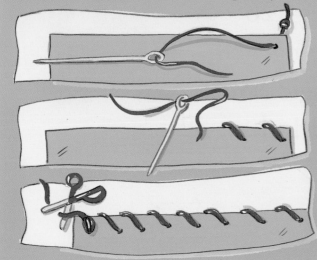

1 Thread needle and knot the end of the thread. Push needle through from the back of the fabric to the front.

2 Loop the needle over the edge and up through the back again. Continue looping round and round, taking slanting stitches.

3 When you reach the end, sew round and round through the last stitch, then cut off the thread.

Art and Craft Skills

Textiles

by Susan Niner Janes

FRANKLIN WATTS
LONDON • SYDNEY

This edition 2004

First published in 1998 by
Franklin Watts,
96 Leonard Street,
London EC2A 4XD

Franklin Watts Australia,
45-51 Huntley Street,
Alexandria, NSW 2015

Copyright © Franklin Watts 1998

Series editor: Kyla Barber
Designer: Lisa Nutt
Illustrator: Lynda Murray
Photographer: Steve Shott
Art director: Robert Walster

A CIP catalogue record for this book
is available from the British Library

ISBN 0 7496 5892 4

Dewey Decimal Classification 746

Printed in Belgium

Franklin Watts and the author wish
to thank the following
manufacturers for supplying craft
materials used in making the
projects in this book:

Ribbons courtesy of Offray Ribbon
Rainbow Felt courtesy of Kunin Felt

Blanket Stitch – to neaten an edge or join two fabrics together at their edges.

1 Thread needle, knot thread end. Bring needle up on front of fabric, then push it back through a little to the right, away from fabric edge.

2 Hold needle straight and pass it through the loop. Keep stitching in this way towards the right, always passing the needle through the loop.

3 Try to space your stitches evenly. When you reach the end, stitch round and round through the last stitch, then cut off thread.

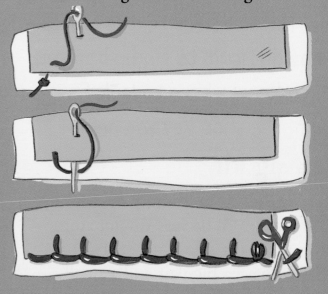

Note: the stitches are shown right-handed: left-handers sew in the opposite direction.

Finishing knot
Tie a knot on the wrong side of the fabric:

Joining knot
To change thread colour as you sew:

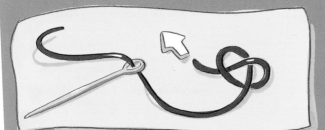

Pinning
To pin fabric to hold it together as you stitch it in place:

⊚ Pin at right angles to the fabric edge, if there is room. The pin points should face inwards.

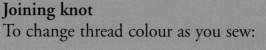

⊚ Remove the pins as soon as you have finished stitching. Put them back in their container – and shut the lid.

⊚ You can also use masking tape or safety pins to hold fabric together temporarily. Sometimes paperclips will work along fabric edges.

Textile supplies

Materials for textile crafts are not difficult to find – but you have to know where to look for them. The shop key will help.

Shop key

Art supply shop

Fabric shop

Supermarket

Craft or DIY shop

Wool shop

Haberdashery counter

Sewing kit

1 Scissors – you need sharp ones for cutting fabric, so be very careful and ask an adult for help if necessary. It is useful to have a big pair and a small pair, so you can handle all sorts of cutting jobs.

2 Pinking shears cut fabric in a zigzag edge and stop it fraying.

3 Safety pins for a safer way to pin.

4 Straight pins can be used for keeping fabrics in place while you are putting your project together.

5 Needles – you will need two types of large-eyed needles: tapestry needles (with blunt tips) and embroidery needles (with pointy tips). Also some ordinary sewing needles. Store needles through a scrap of felt when they are not in use.

Fabric, yarn and thread

6 Felt is a non-woven textile material. It comes in a wide range of colours and will not fray. Some felt is washable.

7 Fabric can be woven, non-woven, knitted, printed or plain. Look for interesting textures and try to recycle old clothes.

8 Net is good for see-through designs; it comes in many colours.

9 Bulky knitting yarn is good for quick results and tapestry wool works well for finer projects.

10 Soft embroidery thread for easy sewing. Use stranded embroidery cotton for details.

Bits and pieces

11 Fibrefill stuffing for soft toy filling ( ).

12 Wadding comes in a flat sheet. Use it as a filling material, for padding ( ).

13 Ribbon – for ties, bows and other decorations ( ).

14 Beads, buttons, sequins and feathers for decoration ( ).

15 Goggle eyes can be glued on soft toys ( ).

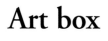

Art box

16 Masking tape can often be used instead of pins ( ).

17 PVA glue can be thinned with water and used as a coating. Remember – it's not washable ( ).

18 Acrylic paints can be used on fabric ( ).

19 A variety of paintbrushes ( ).

20 Cold water dyes: you need a sachet of dye fix for each tin of dye ( ).

21 Fabric paints – always read the label on the jar or tube ( ).

22 Dimensional fabric paint for making raised outlines ( ).

23 Steel ruler for measuring and cutting against ( ).

24 Pencils and rubbers ( ).

25 Paper and card ( ).

26 Sticky putty ( ).

27 Plasticine – for sculpting moulds for fabric mâché ( ).

From the kitchen

Greaseproof paper – low-cost tracing paper ( ).

Dried rice or lentils for filling juggling bags ( ).

Plastic bowl or ice cream tub – dye containers ( ).

Washing-up liquid for cleaning-up ( ).

Plastic drinking straws for curling ribbon ( ).

Table salt used for dyeing ( ).

Plastic food wrap to stop wet material from sticking ( ).

Keep it tidy!

Kitchen roll or rags for wiping spills.
Newspapers – to cover tabletops.
Old clothes – to wear for messy projects.

Ragcraft

Ragcraft projects usually start with strips or scraps. Recycle old clothes and bits of spare material and create something new from something old.

You will need

- three colours of felt
- ribbon
- scraps of fabric
- embroidery needle
- scissors
- net (to match felt)
- soft embroidery thread
- straight pins
- dried lentils or rice
- pencil and ruler

1 For each juggling bag cut two 10 x 10cm squares of felt and two 10 x 10cm squares of net in a matching colour. Then cut small pieces of ribbon, fabric and snippets of embroidery thread.

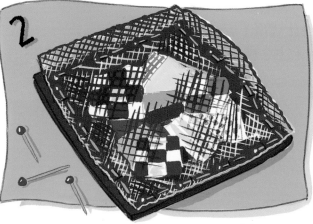

2 Arrange the rag scraps on a felt square. Place a net square over the felt square and pin, then sew, edges together, sandwiching the rag scraps in between. Repeat for the other pieces of felt and net.

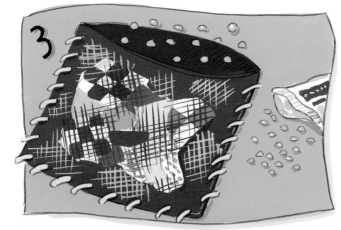

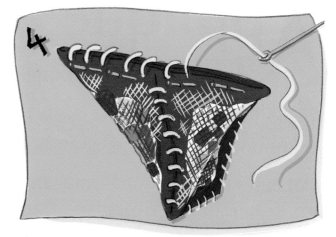

3 Pin the squares together. Oversew three sides, then fill about three-quarters full with dried lentils or rice.

4 Squeeze the two unsewn edges of the bag together so the seams are in the centre. This makes a pyramid shape. Pin in place, then oversew to seal.

Now try these

Rag-Knot Picture Frames

To make a rag-knot, just cut fabric into strips, knot tightly three times, then cut off the tails. This forms a ball. To make up, cut a frame from a cardboard box, then glue lots of knots on to create a pattern.

Rag-Wrapped Bangles

Cut a strip of plastic from a fizzy drink's bottle. Wrap sharp edges with masking tape and tape plastic into a ring. Cut a strip of wadding and glue it on. Cut rag strips and spiral them around to cover the bracelet base, knotting rags to join on new colours.

TEXTILE TIPS

◆ Net can be slippery to use. The easy way to cut net is to stick masking tape on to the net to make the shape, then cut along the tape edges.

◆ Combine plain and patterned rags in your projects. When knotted, patterned rags have a speckled appearance.

◆ Rags are also just what you need for the craft of fabric mâché, see page 20, and for making decorative patches on clothing, see page 11.

Appliqué

Appliqué is a technique of adding patches and trimmings to pictures and clothes. Recycle old material and try this fabric art picture.

1 Plan your design on paper. An appliqué picture is sewn on in layers, so you must think carefully about the shapes of the pieces and the order in which they have to be sewn on.

2 Trace pattern shapes on to some greaseproof paper, then cut them out. Number the greaseproof paper shapes with their sewing order. Pin each one to your chosen fabric, then cut it out.

3rd
2nd
Sew on 1st

3 Pin then sew each piece of fabric on to the background fabric (the blue felt) in the numbered order. Use decorative embroidery stitches, such as oversewing or blanket stitch (see page 5).

4 Add the finishing touches: sew or glue on beads for "apples" and a doorknob; paint the window panes; sew flower stems and sew or glue on button flowers.

Now try these

Patterned Denim

Cut out denim shapes, then wash them to "fur up" the edges. Ask an adult to iron them. Sew patches on and decorate them as shown.

Star T-Shirt

Take an old T-shirt and cut out a star shape in the centre. Wash and dry the T-shirt to fray the cut out edges. Pin a big patch of fabric behind the opening and sew it in place.

TEXTILE TIPS

◎ Appliqué can be glued instead of sewn. Use textile glue, for washable results.

◎ To stop ribbon ends from fraying when you cut them, brush with watered-down PVA glue.

◎ For safer sewing, hold patches in place with safety pins. You need only two or three per patch.

Simple shisha

This method is inspired by the shisha mirror embroidery of India and Pakistan, in which real mini-mirrors are stitched on to fabric.

1 If your metallic card is thin, glue a piece of thick paper on to the back. Draw around a coin to make mirror discs. Cut them out.

2 Place the mirror disc on top of a blob of sticky putty. Push a sharp pencil or nail through each disk four times. The putty will catch the sharp point.

3 Put the mirror disc on backing fabric and hold it in place with your thumb. Bring the needle and thread up from under the fabric and sew through the holes, working your way around the mirror. Tie thread ends at the back.

Backpack and purse

A drawstring bag is a traditional shisha project – you could also add straps to make a backpack. Each bag is made from two felt rectangles – you only have to decorate the front.

What next?

A shape with four centre holes can be stitched on in several different ways:

Now try these

Night Sky Pencil Case

Cut out stars and planets from metallic card. Pierce one hole in the centre of each. Sew into the hole from each edge using metallic thread.

Baseball Cap

Sew shapes on to a baseball cap. You can even create patterned shapes by gluing computer clip art or magazine cuttings on to card and stitching it on.

Textile Tips

★ Curved nail scissors make easy work of cutting out mirror discs (ask permission before using them).
★ To stop your "mirrors" moving as you sew them, stick them in place with PVA glue.

Sock toys

Make soft toys easily and simply by stuffing the toe-end of an old sock and adding stiffened ribbon for hair. Add felt details and goggle eyes to make different characters.

You will need

- old sock
- a 6mm-wide satin ribbon
- goggle eyes
- polyester fibrefill soft toy filling
- dimensional fabric paint
- needle and thread
- drinking straws
- old paintbrush
- felt
- PVA glue
- scissors
- masking tape
- card

1 Cut off the toe end of an old sock. Stuff it, then sew running stitch close to the cut edge. Pull up the thread ends and knot them.

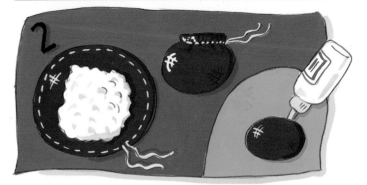

2 For a nose, cut a circle from a sock. Stitch around the edge leaving loose ends and put stuffing in the centre. Pull up the thread, knot the ends and glue in place.

3 For the hair, make stiffened ribbon spirals and zigzags as shown opposite. Cut three pieces of the curly ribbon, cross them at their centres and sew on.

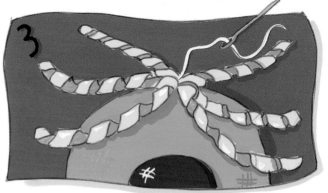

Now try these

Penguins

Make bodies from black socks, then glue on a felt bib, beak, fish, wings, feet and goggle eyes. You can also add a ribbon bow-tie.

Pocket-sized Toys

Cut out a shape in card, cut a piece of wadding the same size and stick it to the card. Cover in the leftover sock material and decorate. Make badges, hair ties or fridge magnets.

TEXTILE TIP

- To stop your sock toy wobbling, stick thick paper to the bottom of the feet.

4 Cut felt pieces for the hands and feet and glue them in place. Hold the felt pieces as the glue dries. Glue on eyes and paint a mouth with fabric paint.

Curly ribbon

For spirals, wind ribbon around a plastic drinking straw (hold ends in place with tape) and brush with water-thinned PVA glue. Let dry. For zigzags, wind ribbon around a 1cm-wide strip of card, which has been covered with plastic food wrap, and brush with water-thinned PVA glue.

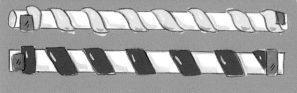

Weaving

These sports' fans are made using needle-weaving on card. You can weave all kinds of thread in this way to create all kinds of effects.

You will need

- ★ wool
- ★ coloured felt
- ★ coloured card
- ★ sticky putty
- ★ dimensional fabric paint
- ★ sharp pencil or nail
- ★ PVA glue ★ paintbrush
- ★ tapestry needle ★ ruler
- ★ pencil
- ★ acrylic paint

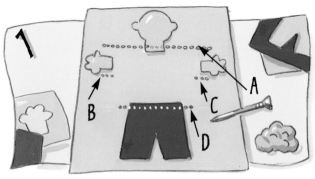

1 Cut out felt head, arms and jeans; glue them on to some backing card. Pierce holes about 5mm apart with a sharp pencil or nail. Pierce 20 holes at A, 3 at B, 3 at C and 14 at D.

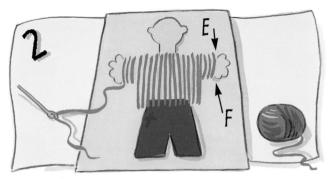

2 Thread a needle with wool, and knot the end. Bring the needle to the front of the card through hole E and back down through F. Continue weaving the wool through all the holes. Knot on the back.

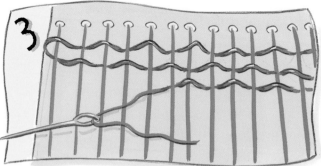

3 Thread the needle and knot the end. Bring the needle up below hole E and weave it "over then under" to the left. Reverse the weaving direction at the row end; weave "under then over" across the second row.

4 Weave until you reach the bottom, then bring the wool to the back and knot it. Glue on felt details – some hair and a badge, and paint on a face.

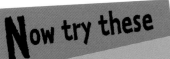

Woven Ribbon

Pin eight rows of ribbons on to the "sticky" side of a piece of iron-on interfacing. Weave eight strands of a different colour of ribbon across them. Sew running stitch around the edges through all the layers to keep them in place. Ask an adult to iron the weaving. Trim the weaving close to the stitching. Tape the woven ribbon behind a card cut-out.

Sporty scarves

Make a scarf in your team colours and attach it to your sports' fan. You can make a scarf out of an old sock, felt, paper, wool or ribbon.

TEXTILE TIP

★ Experiment with different wools, textures and colours.

Friendship chains

Friendship chains are quick and easy to make from simple links. Use small links for bracelets, or larger ones for belts and handles. Experiment with colours, materials and fabrics.

You will need

- ★ felt
- ★ beads (optional)
- ★ scissors
- ★ tracing paper
- ★ pencil
- ★ card
- ★ masking tape
- ★ fine-point pen
- ★ 6mm-wide ribbon
- ★ needle and thread

Link pattern

This is the template for one bracelet-sized chain link. Cut slits on the red lines for plaited-look chains and on the blue lines for disc-link chains. For belt links, enlarge the template.

1 A template for the basic bracelet link is given above. Trace it on to card and cut it out. Draw around this shape end to end five times on a long piece of card. Cut it out and tape it on to a piece of felt.

2 Draw around the card edge with a fine-point pen, and cut out the strip of felt. To cut the strip into links, just snip across at the narrow bit, every two bumps. Repeat using felt of different colours.

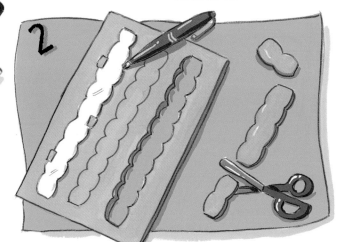

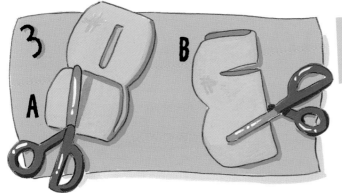

3 For a plaited-look chain, cut the slits as shown above in A. To make a disc-link chain, cut the slits as shown in B.

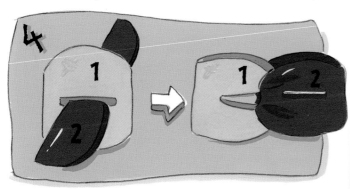

4 Fold link 1 in half widthwise. Fold link 2 in half lengthwise, thread it through slits of link 1. Now spread the two halves of link 2 open and fold them together as you did for link 1. This makes a new link. Repeat to build up your chain. Sew on ribbons, beads or tassels.

Now try these

Neck Purse

For each side of the purse, make three five-link chains. Oversew them together, side-to-side. Pin front and back together and oversew the edges, leaving top open. Sew on a ribbon strap.

Bag Straps

Cut a large rectangle of hessian. Make chain-link straps and sew them on. Fold the hessian in half and sew the sides together. You can fringe the edges of the hessian.

Fabric mâché

Fabric mâché and papier-mâché are similar crafts. Paste small pieces of fabric over a mould or base to build up a shape. Try this lion mask — it's light and slightly bendy.

You will need

- lightweight fabric, cut into small rectangles, about 4cm x 5cm
- plasticine
- a large piece of card
- PVA glue
- acrylic paints
- 30cm of black cord elastic
- paintbrushes (both flat and pointy)
- scissors
- pencil
- plastic food wrap

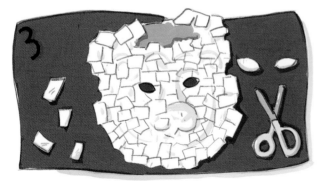

1 Sketch a lion mask on thick card. Build up the nose, mouth and brow areas with plasticine. Cover it all with plastic food wrap.

2 Soak the fabric rectangles in PVA glue thinned with water. Place them on the mask mould one at a time, overlapping them. Shape them to the mould.

3 For the mane, stick fabric pieces to the outer edges of the mask shape. Leave it in a warm place to dry. Lift the mask off the mould and cut out eye holes.

4 Replace the mask on the mould and paint it. Let it dry. Brush on a layer of watery PVA glue for a shiny finish. Pierce holes at the sides and tie on elastic cord.

Now try these

Patchwork Bowls

Cut squares of gingham fabric, and mould them over a plastic food wrap covered-bowl. When the fabric is dry, varnish with PVA glue. Pierce evenly-spaced holes around top. Work blanket stitch or oversewing through the holes.

TEXTILE TIPS

◎ Choose lightweight fabrics to get a slightly see-through effect.

◎ Unlike papier-mâché, a single layer of fabric mâché is all you need. Make sure that fabric pieces overlap without gaps.

Wrapping

Wrapping is where some wool is spiralled around an inner bundle of threads to make a smooth covering. It adds strength and colour to these wool people.

You will need

- bulky wool
- card
- ruler
- scissors
- felt
- dimensional fabric paint
- scissors
- tapestry needle

Wrapping: the basics

1 Make a wool loop as long as the section to be wrapped. Hold the loop in place with your thumb, then bring one wool end under and around the threads you want to wrap.

2 Now spiral the wool around the thread bundle, moving towards the loop.

3 Thread the "wrapping wool" through the loop.

4 Gently tug the bottom wool end until the loop and the wrapping wool are pulled out of sight beneath the wrapping.

5 Snip off the wool tail at top. The wrapping will not come undone.

Simple Tassel

Cut a piece of card. Wrap thread around it, eight times or more. Tie the thread ends tightly at the top and tuck the knot under. Cut through the bottom of the loops to free the tassel from the card.

1 To make woollen dolls, cut a piece of card 15cm long. Wrap yarn around it twenty times. Tie them at the top. Divide the tassel into two bunches of ten yarns for the legs. Tie each bunch tightly at the bottom. Slip the tassel off the card.

2 Start wrapping 2.5cm down from the top of the tassel. Wrap around the whole tassel for the body. In a new colour, wrap one leg then the other.

3 For the arms, cut eight wool strands 15cm long. Thread a needle with one strand and pass it through the body top. Repeat for all the strands then wrap them to make arms.

4 To finish, stuff the head with a bit of crumpled wool. Cut across the loops at the leg bottoms. Trim arm wool. Add wool hair and paint a face with fabric paint.

Now try these

Skipping Rope

Wrap a skipping rope in different colours. Paint the handles and add a wrapped yarn "grip" on each. Decorate with tassels (see page 22).

Beads

To make each bead, cut a strip of felt and fold it in half widthwise. Wrap the centre section, then fringe the bottom edges. Decorate with fabric paint.

Wrap weaving

These colourful weavings are inspired by "Ojos de Dios" or God's Eyes – Mexican folk art symbols believed to bring good luck.

Hexagons

Draw a circle with compasses. Keep the compasses set to the same radius as your circle, then mark six points around the circle edge. Use a ruler and pencil to connect the points.

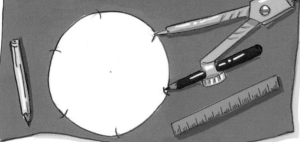

You will need

- ★ bulky wool in different colours
- ★ large-eyed embroidery needle   ★ compass
- ★ sharp pencil or nail   ★ sticky putty
- ★ ruler and pencil   ★ masking tape
- ★ scissors   ★ coloured card

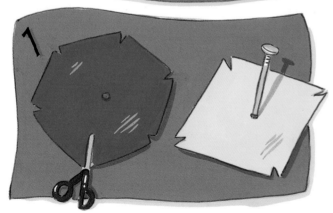

1 Cut squares and hexagons from card. Cut narrow slits in the corners, about 1cm deep. Carefully pierce a hole in the centre of each card.

2 Thread the wool through the slits as shown. The wool should be stretched tight. Tape the ends on to the back of the card.

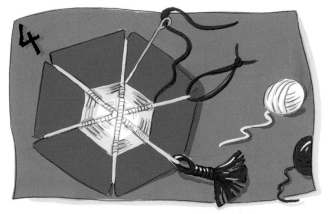

3 Thread a needle with your first colour. Bring it up at the centre, over the crossed yarns in the middle, then back down. Knot on the back. Then bring the wool back up and loop it around each of the fixed wool spokes in turn.

4 To change colours, push the needle through the card at a wool spoke. Tie on a new colour on the wrong side. Thread the needle, bring the wool back through the same hole to the right side, and continue weaving. To finish, tie on tassels (see page 22) and a hanging loop.

"Ojo" colours

Ojo colours have meanings. Yellow stands for the sun god, green represents new life and growth, while blue is the rain god's colour.

Now try these

Holiday Sparkle

Take two cocktail or lollipop sticks, cross them at their centres and bind them together. Using a mixture of metallic and plain thread, weave by looping thread around each stick spoke in turn (no needle required). To finish, tie the end of the wool on to one of the stick spokes. Glue beads on to the stick tips.

Weave a Web

The web is woven like the card weavings, but the wool is spaced apart. Make the creepy crawly from a rolled-up strip of fake fur fabric and pipe cleaners.

Rosettes

Stitch a strip of fabric, pull up the thread and you have a flower-like gathered circle called a rosette. Use rosettes as the building blocks for this bumble bee.

You will need

- 5cm-diameter polystyrene ball (from craft shops)
- yellow felt, black felt
- old black sock
- yellow net
- 50cm of black cord elastic
- 5 black beads
- 2 goggle eyes
- furry pipe cleaners: 2 yellow, 4 black
- stretchy fabric (for nose)
- needle and thread
- pinking shears
- PVA glue
- scrap of red felt (for mouth)

Basic rosette

Cut a strip of felt. For a decorative edge, cut the bottom of the strip with pinking shears. Sew running stitch along the top edge, then pull together the loose ends of the thread to gather up the material.

Bumble bee

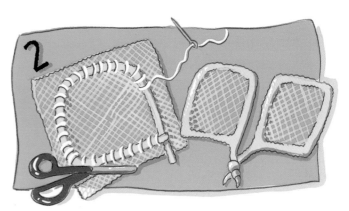

1 To make a head, gather the heel of a sock over a polystyrene ball. Sew on a red nose (see page 14). Sew on pipe cleaner antennae and glue on goggle eyes and a felt mouth. Sew on 50cm of cord elastic to the back of the head.

2 For wings, bend yellow pipe cleaners into loops. Lay them on top of a double layer of yellow net. Sew the net to each wing loop, then trim the edges. Twist wings together at the bottom to make a pair.

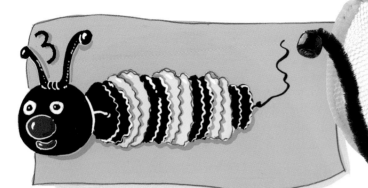

3 Cut 8 black strips (3.5 x 22cm) and 6 yellow (3.5 x 25cm). Make them into rosettes (see "Basic rosette"), and thread them on to the cord elastic in pairs. Alternate yellow and black pairs.

4 Bend three pipe cleaners in half to make three pairs of legs. Slot them between the rosettes and glue them in place.

TEXTILE TIP

☺ To make rosettes out of material other than felt, brush PVA, mixed with water, on to the fabric where you want to cut it. The edge will then be easier to cut and it won't fray.

Now try these

Glitzy Rosette

Make a winner's rosette by sewing net strips in two widths together as one rosette. Top this with a fabric rosette. Add a ribbon tail, sequins and a safety pin fastener at the back.

Flower Garland Scarf

Sew fabric rosettes side by side and add felt leaves and bead "flower centres".

Resist dyeing

Resist dyeing means that patterns are created by stopping dye or paint from soaking into the fabric evenly. Different things can be used to block out areas of colour – here we use tying and masking tape.

You will need

- ★ for each colour: a tin of cold water fabric dye; a sachet of cold water dye fix; and 60g of table salt
- ★ old cotton hankies
- ★ measuring jug
- ★ plastic bowl
- ★ rubber gloves
- ★ tapestry wool
- ★ string and elastic bands
- ★ old spoon
- ★ scissors
- ★ plastic bags and ties
- ★ embroidery needle

1 Make the hankies damp and tie them to make patterns. Spotty: tie in pebbles with thread, very tightly. Stripes: concertina-fold the hankie and wrap it tightly with elastic bands. Bull's eye: pick up the hankie by its centre and crunch it into folds. Tie it tightly from the top down.

DYES ARE POWERFUL CHEMICALS. ASK AN ADULT TO HELP.

2 Ask an adult to prepare the dye solution in a plastic container, and follow the manufacturer's instructions. Dunk the hankies in the dye and squeeze them lightly. After one minute, remove hankies and put them in a plastic bag. Leave overnight.

3 Next day, rinse the hankies under the cold tap until the water runs clear. Cut off the thread or remove the elastic bands. Wash the hankies in hot water mixed with washing-up liquid. Let them dry. Ask an adult to iron them.

4 Parachutes: make wrapped doll skydivers, see page 22. Sew a piece of string on each corner of the hankie. Sew the free end of each string on to the skydiver's back.

Now try these

Masking Tape Resist

Tape a triangle of dry fabric on to a plastic food wrap-covered piece of cardboard. Stick on bits of masking tape, making a pattern. Brush on fabric paint mixed with water. Dry it in sunlight then fix the colour as directed. Make up windsurfs.

Paint magic

Brush it, sponge it, squeeze it on – paints can transform a plain piece of fabric simply and easily.

You will need

- ◆ sew-in interfacing or lightweight fabric
- ◆ dimensional fabric paint   ◆ masking tape
- ◆ fabric paints   ◆ paintbrush   ◆ scissors
- ◆ paper and card   ◆ black felt-tip
- ◆ safety pin   ◆ sticky tape or label   ◆ PVA glue

Which paint?

Fabric paints can be transparent (see-through) or opaque (solid), or dimensional. To select a paint, first decide what effect you want to create, then read the labels to find out which paint can do the job. If you are still not sure which paint to buy, don't guess – ask a shop assistant for advice.

Fat cats

Draw a cat in pencil on some interfacing. Paint the outline using dimensional fabric paint. Next day, colour in the "fur" with fabric paint. For a fuzzy effect, make the fabric damp before you start painting. Glue the cat on to some card and cut it out.

Now try these

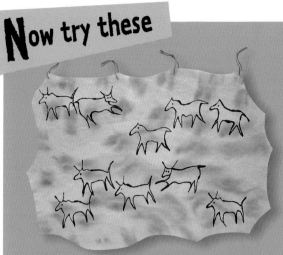

Cave Painting
Paint background on wet fabric using fabric paints. When dry, paint on the animals.

Brilliant Butterflies
Paint butterflies on very wet interfacing. Dot the paint on with a brush – the colour will spread. Try to make both wings match. Dry flat, then paint in the body with 3-D fabric paint.

Apple Bookmark
From a clear plastic folder, snip out an apple and a leaf shape to leave two stencils. Cut a narrow strip of hessian. Tape the apple stencil on to the hessian and dab paint through the opening with a nearly dry brush. Do the apples first then the leaves. Finally, paint on the stems. Cut a piece of felt and sew it to the back of the hessian.

TEXTILE TIPS
◆ Always paint on natural fabrics, like 100% cotton, that have been washed first.

◆ Acrylic paints work well on fabric – but the results will be slightly stiffer than purpose-made fabric paint, and they may not be washable.

◆ Have a go with fabric crayons. Draw your design on paper, then have an adult iron it on to fabric. The flip image prints.

◆ Create an airbrush-like effect: mix creamy paint, then flick it on to fabric using an old toothbrush.

Glossary

appliqué Decorating fabric by attaching patches and trimmings (10–11).

fabric mâché A craft technique in which small pieces of fabric are pasted together over a mould in order to construct a new object (20–21).

friendship bracelet A handmade bracelet, made as a gift. The giver ties it on to the friend's wrist as a symbol of friendship (18–19).

link A piece of a chain that fits together with other pieces that are exactly the same (18–19).

"ojo de Dios" A Mexican good luck symbol, made of yarn wrapped around crossed sticks (24–25).

resist dyeing Any type of fabric decoration in which areas of the fabric are prevented from soaking up dye or paint to make a pattern (28–29).

rosette A circle of fabric made from a strip which has been gathered along one long edge (26–27).

shisha A traditional style of Indian and Pakistani embroidery in which mirror discs are stitched on to fabric (12–13).

wadding A flat, fluffy sheet of fibres, similar to stuffing, which is used as padding (14–15).

weaving A way of making fabric by lacing yarns together. Usually a set of yarns are set up, and then other yarns are inserted through or around them (16–17, 24–25).

wrapping A way of spiralling a piece of yarn around an inner bundle of yarns, making a smooth outer covering (22–23).

Index